the Tropical Fish

A guide to selection, housing, care,

nutrition, health, breeding, species and plants

D1422226

Contents

Contents

Foreword

Keeping an aquarium is in the eyes of very many people a bothersome task. These people think that the hobby is very time-consuming and that you have to know a lot about chemistry and fish to understand what you are dealing with. But this is not completely true. The hobby demands just as much time as you are prepared to invest. There are fans who daily spend more than two hours with their aquarium, but if you only do the absolutely necessary, then you do not need to spend as much time on your tank.

And difficult? Well, different people have differing opinions about this. Compare your aquarium with keeping a dog. Do you really know all there is to know about a dog's health? Do you know exactly what diseases your dog can come in contact with and what you must do about them? Your answer is probably "no". You do not have to know, if it is sick, you take him to a specialist, such as a vet.

The same is also true, more or less, of an aquarium. The more you know about it the easier it all is. But if you have basic knowledge such as is given in this book, then you are well equipped to have a flourishing beginner's aquarium in your living room. Many aquarium keepers are members of aquarium clubs. If you have a problem, which you really cannot solve, then you can ask the experts in the club. That is why it is wise to join the local aquarium club. You can get help there with all your questions and problems. Moreover, what is nicer than chatting about your hobby with other fans?

About Pets

Discus *(Symphysodon discus)*

A Publication of About Pets.

ISBN 1852792272
First printing
September 2003
Second printing
May 2004

Original title: *de Startersgids aquarium*
© 2000 - 2002 Welzo Media Productions bv,
About Pets,
Warffum, the Netherlands
http://www.aboutpets.info

Photos:
Frans Maas, Rob Doolaard,
and Kingdom Books

Editor: Karen Wolters

Printed in China

In advance

Before you go to the shop to buy your aquarium products you will already have had to make a good deal of decisions. What sort of aquarium do you want? Tropical, saltwater, freshwater? Do you have specific wishes as far as the fish and plants are concerned?

Angel Fish
(Pterophyllum scalare)

Not all fish get on with each other and it would of course be annoying if your fish were to eat each other up. And have you thought about the different materials? Do you want a plastic aquarium or rather one made of glass? There may be many more questions to be considered and decisions to be made. In order to reach a considered choice you can use the information from this chapter.

Types of aquariums
The appearance of an aquarium is determined to a large degree of course by the fish and the plants that are in it. It is logical that taste plays a key role here. Do you put plants in your aquarium, for example, which you find completely ugly? Probably not. Yet you cannot choose only nice

plants and beautiful fish. You must first look and see if the plants and animals go together well. The composition of the water is also important. A saltwater fish will be floating belly up in no time if it has to swim in fresh water. Conversely only a few plants thrive in salt water. So first try to define what sort of aquarium you would like to have. To help you with this, we give you some suggestions here.

Tropical aquarium
The tropical aquarium consists of fish and plants, which are originally to be found in the tropical countries around the equator. Many beginners choose such a tropical aquarium. The best known fish is probably the guppy, although not many people know that

this fish belongs in a tropical aquarium. Other possible inhabitants for a community tank are tetras, swordbearers, small bass and tropical shrimps. In a tropical aquarium you always need a filter and a heater. The temperature of the water is a minimum of 23 °C. Most fish can be kept at a temperature of 24-26 °C and the plants can also just about survive at this temperature. Although, in principle, all sizes of tank are suitable for a tropical aquarium, it is advisable not to buy too small a tank. An aquarium of about 80 centimetres is easier to keep under control than a shorter tank.

Freshwater aquarium

A freshwater aquarium can be tropical but not necessarily. The name 'freshwater aquarium' means no more than that the plants and animals in this aquarium live in fresh water in their original environment. In your freshwater aquarium, you try to imitate this as well as possible.

Saltwater aquarium

A saltwater aquarium is usually not the first choice for a beginner. For example, it can sometimes take a year before your aquarium is complete. Apart from the aspect of patience the keeping of sea creatures is not simple. Should you nevertheless wish to start with this, then we advise you not to put fish in your aquarium from the beginning, but first the so-called "lower species". Consider, for example, anemones and shrimps. Just as in the case of the other aquariums, not all animals get on with each other and sound prior investigation is therefore also

Ornate Tetra
(Hyphessobrycon bentosi rosaceus)

White Cloud
(Tanichthys albonubes)

important. Additionally, a salt-water aquarium is often a good deal more expensive than a tropical aquarium.

Cold water aquarium

A cold water aquarium is usually not the first choice for a novice aquarium keeper. But there are people who have a pond outside in their garden and who also want to have something to look at in the winter. The difficult thing about a cold water aquarium in the house is the fact that you have to keep the water at the right temperature. That can be very difficult when your central heating is running at full blast in the winter. If the water gets too warm, the fish and other animals can die through lack of oxygen. In

a cold water aquarium you can keep little (koi) carps or goldfish, although it is then important that you do not put too many plants in with them. The reason is that your fish will soon have conquered these plants and that causes serious water pollution. However, you can also decide to work more with plants in a cold water aquarium, perhaps complemented with domestic varieties of fish.

Special aquarium

A special aquarium is a tank that is specially set up for a particular sort of fish or for a particular biotope. Such an aquarium demands a lot of specific knowledge and this is one of the reasons why it is not really suitable for the beginner.

Guppy

A special aquarium often becomes a combination of an aquarium with a terrarium, which therefore has a separate land section. Aquariums that belong to the category "special aquarium" are amongst others the South America aquarium, the Malawi aquarium and the Tanganyika aquarium. A cichlid aquarium is a special aquarium. This is a tank with lots of stones in it. We advise you as a beginner not to keep cichlids. These - fantastic - fish need very special attention. You must therefore specialise.

What shapes of aquariums are there?

Although by far most aquariums still have the standard rectangular form, some manufacturers play somewhat more with the possible shapes. When you are buying an aquarium, always consider if the build of the tank suits your interior surroundings. Try to judge this in advance. Once you have set up your aquarium, you will not want to empty it again so quickly and it would be a shame if you were not able to enjoy it at its best.

There are more and more corner tanks on sale. The advantage of these aquariums is that they take up less space because they fit perfectly into a corner. In addition they have a spatial effect.

In general square aquariums are not so popular because you can get a rectangular tank for the same money. You will also notice that they are rarely offered for sale in the shops.

There is a growing number of column aquariums ("tall tanks") on sale, some finished more beautifully than others. However, this form of aquarium has a large disadvantage. It only has a small water surface and that means that relatively little oxygen can enter the water. It is almost superfluous to tell you that animals in the aquarium will die if there is not enough oxygen.

What is the best size and place for my aquarium?

The size of your aquarium depends in the first instance on the size of the room in which you want to place your aquarium. Where do you have space? Whatever decision you make, make sure that direct sunlight can never shine through the windows into the aquarium. So a place directly in front of a sliding door is fundamentally wrong. Try also to avoid the aquarium standing next to a door. The fish can get used to the many movements around the door, but a door that is not closed gently enough causes vibrations. This can cause stress to your fish, which can kill them.

The aim is that you should soon be able to enjoy the fascinating underwater world, so it is probably a good idea to go and sit in your favourite chair in order to determine the place for the aquarium.

Cichlid

Marbled Hatchetfish
(Carnegiela strigata)

The golden rule is that you must not let your aquarium dominate your living environment. Make sure that you can look into the centre of the tank from your favourite spot so that you have a view of all animals both on the surface and on the ground.

When you have determined the place, you must choose a strong stand. An empty aquarium may not weigh much. However once it has been filled with water, the stand will have to support quite a weight. An aquarium that can hold 45 litres of water can easily weigh 55 kg. Not only must the aquarium stand be strong, the same is true of course for the floor. A concrete floor usually does not cause any problems but a wooden floor has to be well supported with beams in the area where the aquarium will stand. Also do not make the mistake of putting your aquarium on two supports with just a plank over them. You will then not be the first to find out that the floor of an aquarium can split. Apart from the damage caused by the water (and the cost that this entails) all your work will have been for nothing. So make sure that your stand is firm and stable and that the weight of the aquarium can be evenly distributed on it. Many ready-made aquariums have a splendid surround in which you can hide parts of your aquarium such as cables. Also make sure that your aquarium is level.

You can of course decide not to stand your aquarium, but to hang it on the wall. This gives a very particular spatial effect. But make sure that the wall can bear the weight of the aquarium. Construction skills are needed for this and for that reason hanging an aquarium is not advisable.

Insurance

If you wish to place a large aquarium in your room, it is a good idea to check your insurance papers. If the tank were to fall, tip over or be knocked over, then you would have enormous (water) damage. Check if you are insured against this. If this is not the case, then it is wise to amend your insurance accordingly.

New or second-hand aquarium?

You can buy a new aquarium at a pet shop. A good pet shop will have several standard models for sale. If you have special wishes, however, then it is advisable to go to a firm that specialises in building aquariums. If you buy a new ready-made aquarium you usually have a limited choice. There are aquarium manufacturers who can completely fulfil your wishes as far as your choice of material and colour is concerned. After all it has to fit in your interior surroundings.

So-called frame aquariums were formerly sold but that does not happen any more. Aquariums are

now made completely out of glass. If you do not want this, you can choose a polyester aquarium that can also be delivered with only a front pane made of glass. This is advisable for people starting with a seawater aquarium. The advantage of a new aquarium is that it is ready-made. The disadvantage, however, is that it is also fairly expensive. The great advantage of a second-hand aquarium is clear. The price is considerably lower than the price of a new one. But you must not let yourself be led by this. If you choose a second-hand aquarium you have to pay attention to a few important details. First try to find out how old the aquarium is. This

is because silicon putty is used in the production of an aquarium. In the 1970's and 80's the quality of this putty was guaranteed for ten years. From 2000 the composition of the putty has been improved and now there is a guarantee of about 30 to 40 years. If the putty is no longer in order, your aquarium will leak and that is not, of course, what you want.

Additionally you have to check if the holders for the fluorescent lights in the hood are glued. If this is the case you must check if you can keep these clean. Dirty cover panes or fluorescent light holders reduce the light level by 40 to 50% and that would be a pity.

Platy

Rummy-Nose Tetra
(Hemigrammus
rhodostomus)

Thermometer

Also check well if the front pane is scratched. Scratches disturb the view. You must take a good look at this in advance, because once you have set up your aquarium you will not want to empty it again so quickly. If there are scratches on it, you can consider having a new front pane put in.

Polyester aquarium

A polyester aquarium resembles the classic aquarium. In the past, the rear wall, the floor and the sidewalls were made out of plate steel and sometimes out of stainless steel. Only the front pane was made of glass. The polyester aquarium looks very much like

this, but it does not rust. It is often delivered with a primer coat and it is lightweight compared to steel. This type of aquarium is maintenance-free and it is not as easily damaged as an aquarium that has glass on all sides. If you want to buy a large tank, a polyester aquarium is worth considering. The prices do not vary much. If your tank has to be smaller than 1.5 metres, it is usually more economical to buy a glass aquarium.

Lighting

Most beginners buy a second-hand aquarium or they decide on a ready-made tank from the pet shop. These aquariums usually already have a lighting hood. Make sure that this is not made of metal, which is often the case with older aquariums. Metal has a conducting function and in view of the fact that we are dealing with water and electricity, the chance of getting a shock is relatively high. Modern lighting hoods are made of plastic and the lighting is incorporated in them. Unfortunately, many manufacturers forget to add ventilation slats, which greatly increases the likelihood of condensation in the hood.

Heating

Most aquariums are delivered with a heating element. If your aquarium does not have this, you will have to buy a source of heat. Pay attention to the amount of heat needed. The output of an aquarium with measurements 60x30x30 cm must be 35-40 watts. Consult your (aquarium) dealer. In the case of a new heating element you also have the choice of various models.

Floor heating is installed on the floor before the sand or gravel floor is added. You can compare it with underfloor heating in a house, but floor heating in an aquarium is connected to the electricity supply by means of a transformer. The advantage of floor heating is that the warmth is distributed evenly and some plants

really like having "warm feet". The disadvantage is that the heating is difficult to reach in the event of a broken wire. It is also relatively expensive.

You can also decide on filter heating, in which the filter pumps contain a heating element. At the top of the pot there is a spiral which heats the water as it passes by, so you need not have a separate element in the aquarium itself and it is easy to keep clean. But if the pump is broken, you immediately have no more heating. A simple air bubble can also block the water flow, and therefore stop the heating from working. The most common source of heat is the heater that you just hang into the aquarium.

Filter

Place the element horizontally against the rear wall and keep it a little off the ground. In this way you will get the highest possible output. You must hang the thermostat in such a way that you do not get a false reading. Some heating elements you can only hang vertically in the aquarium so that the setting button remains above the water. Pay attention to this when buying the heating element. The advantage of this type of heating is that it is relatively cheap. The disadvantage is that you must camouflage the heater very well to avoid an unsightly effect.

Vacuum cleaner for your tank

All about aquariums and water chemistry

Meanwhile, you have reached the stage that you have your eye on a particular aquarium and perhaps you already have it at home.

But an empty tank is far from being an aquarium. Before you can set up the tank and can go and buy fish and plants you must first know something about the floor of the aquarium. In addition, the aquarium must also be filled with water. That means that you must also have a good knowledge of water and its composition. Prior knowledge about water can prevent many problems.

The walls of an aquarium

For a long time it was all the rage to cover the walls of the aquarium with posters, which were, of course, fixed to the outside of the glass. In the meantime these posters have completely gone out of fashion. Some people decide not to cover their aquarium from the inside. We advise against this for

two reasons. First, it sometimes looks very odd if you can see the wallpaper through the aquarium. Second, transparent walls can reflect the surroundings too much. This can be an enormous source of stress for your fish. Remember that when you choose the walls of your aquarium you are determining the exterior appearance of this aquarium for a long time. That is why most aquarium keepers choose a calm background which appears as natural as possible.

Ready-made synthetic walls

In shops you can buy synthetic rear walls. The great advantage of these walls is that they cannot rot and disintegrate. They are usually made of polystyrene, which is coloured throughout. So if the wall is slightly damaged, the damage can scarcely be seen. Compare this to synthetic walls, which are only coloured on the outside. If a fish nibbles at the wall, you will see an annoying white mark straight away. Synthetic walls have a surface that appears natural, into which materials that we also meet in nature - leaves or twigs, for example - have been pressed or poured. The disadvantage of these panels is that they often have a shiny surface, which appears unnatural. You can avoid this by roughening the surface a little with a steel brush.

Cork walls

Cork is becoming an increasingly popular material. How many people now have a cork floor in their living room? It is also popular with aquarium owners. Most aquarium walls made of pressed cork can be bought in fixed sizes. This size is often 100 x 50 cm. The great advantage of these brown-coloured rear walls is that they give your aquarium a natural look. Cork itself is a natural product and that means that it is susceptible to disintegration. After a number of years, your cork wall will disintegrate and you will have to put in a new one.

Fixing the walls

It is best to use a dark silicone sealant for fixing the rear and side walls. Ask for it in the shop where you buy the walls. Make sure that there is no dirt between the walls and the glass because this can be a culture medium for blue algae. (See also chapter Algae.) Experienced aquarium owners do not fix the whole wall to the glass but just fix it at the top to the stabiliser. The upwards pressure of the water keeps the walls perfectly in their place. However, make sure that the rear walls join the side walls seamlessly.

Checker Barb
(Barbus oligolepis)

The substrate

Plants grow according to the law of the minimum. That means that they only need a little of all the necessary nutrients but that all nutrients must be present. If one is missing, the plant will lose its balance and can die. When buying substrate you must take into account the fact that plants need everything but in very small amounts. There are so many different kinds of substrate for sale which are really too rich in nutrients. Because the plants cannot process the nutrients in time, the substrate starts to rot. Gas bubbles develop, which cause the plants to uproot and fish to die. If you want to be on the safe side, you can make gravel yourself out of mortar sand or river sand. You can perhaps add to this with turf or fine pebbles. These can be bought at any pet shop. Rinse the pebbles clean and free of dust before you put them in your aquarium. Go for stones with a dark colour because fish prefer a dark substrate.

Odessa Barb
(Barbus odessa)

Half-Striped Penguin
(Thayeria ifati)

Building up a substrate

Oxygen is the fuel for bacteria and these are essential for your aquarium. This is why your floor should not be compacted because there is then no room left for oxygen and gas to escape. When building up the floor it is best to begin with sprinkling little pieces of turf. For this, use garden turf that you can buy in a specialist aquarium shop. Turf that you buy at a garden centre sometimes contains insecticides or fertilisers and these must be avoided. Saw the turf into slices that are one centimetre thick. Then break the slice into pieces of about 5 centimetres and sprinkle these pieces onto the substrate. After this, sprinkle the sand on top of it. In unwashed river sand there is a little bit of clay, which contains enough of the bacteria needed. Put the washed pebbles on top of the sand until you have a layer of about two centimetres. If you use turf, you must first soak it in water for at least a week. By doing this you prevent the turf from floating.

Filling the tank

When the walls and the floor are in the aquarium you can put water in it. Tip: put a (clean) rubbish bag on the floor of the tank. This prevents the water from going murky straight away. When the water is completely still, you can then simply remove the bag.

Water

Simple as the word may be, it can be complex in the aquarium

Clown Loach
(Botia macracanthus)

world. Water is a simple little thing that consists of two parts hydrogen and one part oxygen. What can possibly be the problem? You would not be the first person to fill up your aquarium tank with tap water and then after some time to look in surprise into the aquarium to see that one fish after the other is dying. Even the plants seem to be giving up. It is therefore wise to learn this or that about water and the chemistry of water before you fill your aquarium. It is time for another chemistry lesson.

The water quality of your aquarium

Do you know what the quality of the water is that comes out of your tap? You can get this

information from your water company. It is important to know the water quality so that you can see how much you will have to adjust the water. For this book we are basing this on the composition for a tropical aquarium (community tank). In their original environment, the inhabitants of your aquarium are used to a different composition and quality of water than that offered by your water company. Take for example the water in the Amazon. To understand the readings, we have to know, among other things, the conductivity. In other words, the ions, which can conduct an electrical current from point A to point B. The conductivity of the water in the Amazon region is about 30 microSiemens (μS). This is also dependent on the time of year. Tap water has a conductivity that varies between 400 and 1200 microSiemens. This is of course an enormous difference.

For your fish this means that they have to live in a very polluted environment compared with their original habitat. These high readings are caused by calcium, salts, metals, minerals and other substances in our drinking water. For us humans it is not harmful, in an aquarium, however, it usually causes problems. It is best to let the water in a community tank vary between 350 and 450 microSiemens. This means that you will have to "treat" the tap

Beautiful Scaled Characin (*Copella natteri*)

water. It is also particularly difficult to have your aquarium water vary between 350 and 450. Even very experienced aquarium owners still have problems with it.

Osmosis water

In some specialist aquarium shops you can have your tap water tested so that you know if you can use it in your aquarium. You can also buy so-called "osmosis" water in most specialist pet shops. This is normal tap water that has already been filtered. Of course you can also go as far as buying an osmosis device, but this is not necessary in the beginning. Apart from osmosis water you can sometimes buy demineralized water. All minerals have been filtered out of this tap water. Aquarium clubs sometimes also sell osmosis water and demineralized water. Find out by getting in touch with a local club. If, for whatever reason, you only have access to tap water, remember that your choice of plants and animals is limited.

Drip method

There is a method of preparing your fish for life in an aquarium filled only with tap water. This functions as follows: Put the new fish with their water in a bucket next to the aquarium. Then hang a pipe in the aquarium and the other end in the bucket. Now let water drip into the bucket. NB: the water must drip very slowly. In this way the fish will slowly get used to the aquarium water. After some time, you can carefully transfer the fish to the aquarium.

Lake Malawi Cichlid
(Pseudotropeus
zebra)

Chocolate Gourami
(Sphearichthys
osphromeoides)

Throw the water from the bucket away. If you buy fish in a pet shop, the sales person will very likely advise you to hang the bag with the fish in your aquarium before you empty it out in your aquarium. However there is the risk that the water in the bag contains harmful bacteria or diseases. You want to keep these out of your aquarium of course. With the drip method you prevent the water that is delivered with your fish getting into your aquarium and yet the fish can still slowly get used to your water.

The pH-value of the water

The pH-value of the water must be in balance. This means that you have to have a value of about 7 pH. You can adjust the value yourself by adding carbon dioxide, but if you do not feel at home in chemistry we advise you not to do this. A simpler method is to soak a few pieces of turf for a few hours in some osmosis water. In any case it is best to get advice from a specialist shop or from an aquarium club.

Temperature

The temperature of the water in a community tank should vary between 23 and 26 °C. This is also dependent on the types of inhabitants.

Carbonate hardness (KH)

The carbonate hardness of your tap water consists mainly of minerals such as calcium and salts. It is important to know a few things here, because it is one of the main reasons for having to regularly change your water. Every fish urinates three times its body weight daily. Uric acid can completely dissolve the carbonate hardness and that is not good. The opposite is also bad for your aquarium: If the KH-value becomes too high, a shortage of carbon dioxide gas can develop. You can imagine the consequences. So try to keep the KH-values for your tropical aquarium between 3-6 KH, then you will always be okay.

Thick-Lipped Gourami
(*Colisa labiosa*)

Calcium and magnesium salts

The total amount of calcium and magnesium salts is called Gh. It is a nutrient for plants and animals and also very important for the skeletal development of a fish, for example. If the Gh-value of your water is wrong, you can often see this by looking at your snails. Their houses are then completely white, which means that they are suffering from calcium deficiency. Ask for advice at your specialist shop or aquarium club.

White's Pearlfish
(*Cynolebias whitei*)

Iron

We human beings need iron. If we have an iron deficiency, we suffer anaemia and we have to swallow tablets to bring our iron levels back to normal. Plants also need iron. They only need minuscule amounts but nevertheless iron is absolutely vital for your aquarium plants. Among other things, it helps the plants to maintain their fresh green or red colour. If you notice that your plants are becoming yellow, that can mean that they have an iron deficiency. If that is the case you must add iron to the water yourself. Do this on a daily basis because the iron rusts owing to the presence of oxygen. It then disintegrates and the plants can no longer absorb it. You can get iron at a pet shop.

Black Molly

Carbon dioxide
If a plant does not get any carbon dioxide it will eventually die. That is why it is important that you make sure that you have enough plants in your aquarium. Plants react strongly to light. During the day plants inhale carbon dioxide

Parrot Platy

and at night they exhale oxygen. This is an important process for your aquarium. It is also the reason why you have to maintain a day and night rhythm in your aquarium. If you have a light shining on your tank for 20 hours a day, the plants will only inhale carbon dioxide. The time to produce oxygen is then too short and your plants will wither in the course of time.

Oxygen
No plant, no animal and of course no human being can live without oxygen. Together with carbon dioxide it forms the circle of life. If you do not have an overpopulation of fish (or other animals) and have enough plants in your aquarium, you do not need to worry about the oxygen content.

If you notice that the fish keep coming to the surface to breathe, however, then something is wrong. The best thing to do is to move the surface of the water with an (air) pump, for example. In this way, the oxygen gets the chance to be absorbed. The most important thing of course is that you find out the reason for the oxygen deficiency. It could be that there are too many bacteria of the wrong type in your tank. Bacteria are important in an aquarium. They ensure that waste products (e.g. fish excrement) are converted into nutrients. In so doing the bacteria use a great deal of oxygen. If there are too many bacteria there will soon be an oxygen deficiency.

Nitrate, nitrite and ammonia

The nitrate content in the water can rise when plants rot. But it can also rise because of waste products of fish. In short, it is always present in your aquarium. If the nitrate content becomes too high, it can turn into nitrite. This is a very poisonous substance that can ensure that your hobby is not long-lived. However an aquarium cannot do without nitrate. It is the end product of bacteria and plants cannot live without this nutrient. It is advisable to let the water stand in the tank for three weeks before the fish are put into a new aquarium. This is also called the "ripening" of an aquarium. Ammonia is also dangerous for fish, certainly if there is too much

in the water. If that is the case, then the water must be changed as quickly as possible. In this way you will get rid of harmful substances, and superfluous nutrients will also be removed.

That is enough introduction to the chemistry of water. But in addition to chemistry it is also good that you should know a few things about biology. Most of this appears in the following chapters, for example in the chapters about plants and fish. However, we have already used a few biological terms. Here is some clarification:

Biotopes

A biotope is the original habitat of an animal. Every biotope has a limited number of plants and creatures. It is important for your animals that you know their biotope well, so that you can imitate this as closely as possible in your aquarium. You must know where your fish come from, which plants grow in the biotope and what else can be found in the animal's habitat. If you completely recreate a specific biotope with your aquarium we call such a tank a "special aquarium".

Lower species

The animate world is split up in two parts and one of those is the order of lower animals. All molluscs belong to this order. That means that snails, starfish and shrimps belong to this category.

The fish

An aquarium is for fish, at least most of them are. Fish definitely are the main concern in our typical aquarium (tropical community tank). Perhaps you already have an idea which fish you want to have in your aquarium.

Lemon Tetra
(Hyphessobrycon pulchripinnis)

It is important that you know a little about the species, apart from just their names, before you make your purchase. In this chapter you will be given basic knowledge about fish and tips for purchase, before we conclude with an overview of fish which are well suited to a tropical aquarium.

Where does the fish swim?
Perhaps this is a strange question, but do you know where the fish you like enjoys swimming most? It is very important to know this. You want to be able to admire a well-filled aquarium and then it would be a shame if it turned out that you had only bought fish that swim at the bottom of the tank. There are three water layers in an aquarium: The surface, the middle and the bottom.

These water layers are defined by the fish that live in them. A sheatfish, for example, is a typical bottom fish. With its snout it tries to find all kinds of tasty things on the ground. You can often tell by looking at fish what kind of swimmers they are. If the snout of the fish points to the top, it is a surface fish.
If the snout points down, then the fish gets its food from the ground. Fish that swim in the middle of an aquarium have their snout pointing to the front.

Fish in flowing water
Sturdily built fish with powerfully developed fins, which also have a large tail, are fish that in their natural habitat live in flowing water. Usually these are fish that live in open water and form large

schools. If you buy such fish you must ensure that there is enough room for them to swim and that your aquarium also has a current.

Fish which live amongst the plants

Fish that always live amongst plants in their own biotope like gently flowing water. These fish can usually swim very fast and they use the plants for shelter. You can recognise these fish by their shape because they are usually torpedo-shaped. Another indicator is the presence of horizontal stripes on the fish.

Fish which live in schools

Before you buy fish it is best to consult an encyclopaedia about the types of fish. You will then know immediately whether the fish you have your eye on is a "school" fish or not. Fish that live in schools cannot flourish if they are kept alone in an aquarium.

Therefore you should buy a school. This is better for the fish and moreover it makes your aquarium look fantastic. A school of fish consists of a minimum of twelve. Of course you can buy solitary fish separately. These are fish that prefer to live without those of their own kind. There are a few types of fish that are best kept as pairs, but to go into this would involve too much detail for this little book. Get advice from your pet shop.

How many fish in your aquarium?

This question is second in importance only to using the correct water. It is easy to overpopulate your aquarium. Many beginners make the mistake of being too enthusiastic about buying fish and they forget to consider the size of the grown fish. School fish and solitary fish are thrown willy-nilly into the tank

Pumpkinseed Sunfish
(Lepomis gibbosus)

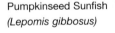

Guppy

Pristella Tetra
(Pristella maxillaris)

and the owner is often surprised that all is not well with his aquarium. Yes, you may well have done all the right things, including getting the composition of the water and its temperature right, yet everything can go wrong when it comes to choosing the fish.

You must at all times avoid overpopulation. If an aquarium is overpopulated, too many waste products are set free, which cannot be processed. Additionally there is only a limited supply of oxygen, which then has to be shared with too many others. Problems begin to occur. The size of your tank determines how many fish you can put in it. There is a method to work this out: Every fish needs about 3 litres of water. First calculate how much water fits into your aquarium. An example: There are 54 litres of water in an aquarium with the measurements

60 x 30 x 30 cm. Now divide 54 by 3. Answer: 18. That means that you can put about 18 grams of fish in this tank. That does not seem like much, but many fish only weigh 1-2 grams. You have, however, not finished when you have worked out the total number of fish. You must also bear the mobility of the fish in mind.

Buying fish

When you have finally made a choice, you can go and look in the shop to see if they sell the fish you want. Sometimes you can also buy fish at aquarium clubs. Never buy too impulsively and always find out how long the fish have already been in the tanks. Pay attention to the following points:
- Do the fish make a healthy impression? Apart from a generally healthy impression, it is also important that you can see if the fins are in good condition.

- How do the fish deal with others of their kind? Fish also have a pecking order, although this is more clearly defined in some types. The dominant fish is the leader and it is often a male. The most withdrawn fish often is at the bottom of the hierarchy. Yet this can change quickly if the composition of the group is altered.
- Does the excrement look nice and brown and compact? If the excrement looks different and suspicious, this can be an indication of an intestinal parasite or a worm disease. Do not buy this fish.
- Does the fish have bright eyes? If the eye of a fish makes a filmy impression, this can mean that the cornea is damaged. Such damage can occur relatively easily if the fish has hit against the walls of the aquarium when being caught or when reacting in a startled way. You must pay special attention to ensure that one eye is not fatter than the other. This can be an indication of a tuberculosis infection, which is very contagious. Humans can also become infected.

Fish and stress

Fish hate nothing more than stress. However you cannot avoid it completely. Each time you transport them, it causes them a great deal of stress, but how else are you going to get your aquarium filled? Your fish is usually sold in a plastic bag. Use the drip method to transfer your fish to your aquarium (see chapter All About Aquariums and Water Chemistry). There is always a difference in the composition and the temperature of the water and that causes stress for the fish. Remember that every change is a stress situation for a fish. It is well known that stress affects the immune system of the fish, which makes it more susceptible to disease and parasites.

Groups of fish

All fish can be subdivided into different groups. It would go too far to deal thoroughly with all these groups in this little book, but we do not want to keep some basic information from you. We shall discuss the following terms: live-bearing, egg-depositing, labyrinth fish and bubble-nest builders.

Live-bearing fish

You will probably think of mammals when you hear the term 'live-bearing'. The term has a completely different meaning when we are dealing with fish, however. Live-bearing fish also lay eggs. The term live-bearing in this context refers to the fact that the young are already completely developed in the egg. At the moment when the egg leaves the mother's body, it discards its shell and the fish is "born".

Gold Barb *(Barbus schuberti)*

Egg depositors

Egg depositors are fish that do not look after their hatch. They often lay their eggs on flat stones and leave them. An example of these are barbs.

Labyrinth fish

Labyrinth fish have an organ in their head that has the shape of a labyrinth. This organ functions as a support for the gills. Labyrinth fish regularly swim to the surface, take a breath of air there and swim back down. The extra air is stored in the intestines. It enables the fish to survive in water that is low in oxygen. Some fish have perfected this system to such a degree, that they are able to crawl over land to another source of water. Because labyrinth fish stick their heads out of the water now and again, it is important that the airflow above the aquarium has about the same temperature as the water in the aquarium. If there is a constant draught above the aquarium, the fish can have great health problems, comparable with pneumonia. You can tell this by looking at the forehead of the fish. It becomes very clearly delineated. The fish also becomes inactive and in the end it will not survive.

Bubble-nest builders

Most labyrinth fish are also bubble-nest builders. You will probably have seen a nest in someone else's aquarium: Sticky foam floats on the water surface. If you see it in your own aquarium, do not remove it. The bubble-nest builders need it during mating. It functions as follows. Bubble-nest builders blow bubbles in which there is a sticky layer of saliva. They take these bubbles to the surface, putting bits of plants and dirt from the bottom of the aquarium in them on the way. A male usually takes a whole night to build a nest. A nest can sometimes protrude several centimetres above the surface of the water. The male courts the female and in a tight embrace he presses the eggs out of her. At the same time fertilisation takes place. Most eggs rise directly and land in the nest between the foam bubbles. Eggs that go down to the bottom are picked up as soon as possible and spat into the nest. The female's role is then over and the male looks after and guards the nest. When the young emerge, they initially live from their yolksac and after that from minuscule little animals which are present in the nest because of rotting plants and dirt from the bottom. When the young come out of the nest, the male often begins work on a new foam nest straight away.

Types of fish

We will now discuss a few types of fish that can often be found in a tropical aquarium. The scope of this little book does not allow us to deal with all types of fish. If you really want to have a serious go at this hobby, it is a good idea to buy a comprehensive fish encyclopaedia.

The guppy

In spite of its fragile appearance the guppy is the king amongst live-bearing fish. The guppy is renowned for its fascinating colours. No two males are identical as far as markings and colour are concerned. The females are often somewhat more soberly

coloured. Guppies live in schools and they demand little of the aquarium. However, a tank with guppies in it also needs several plants among which they can hide. Guppies are sometimes also called "million fish".

Platies

Platies are also little fish, which are now bred in several "models". They have all been given different names, but the original Latin name is still *Xiphophorus platy*. Like guppies, they are live-bearing fish which swim in schools. The platy is an enormously popular tropical fish, which is easy to keep. It can be recommended very strongly for you as a beginner.

Tetras

The tetra family is very large, that is why we will only deal here

Platy
(Xiphophorus maculatus)

Neon Tetra
(Paracheirodon innesi)

Guppy, male

Cardinal Tetra
(Paracheirodon
axelrodi)

Swordtails

This fish from Central America can grow to as long as 10 centimetres and is therefore not suitable for a small aquarium. It is, however, not a difficult fish to keep and can be bought in several different "models". Some swordtails are red or orange and others are yellow or green. There is something for everybody. The species is called swordtail because the males are "equipped" with a long sword. Swordtails require a closely planted corner in the aquarium. They prefer to swim in the middle layer and you can even sometimes catch this fish swimming backwards. They are very fast swimmers, which now and again shoot through the aquarium. If you choose a swordtail, you must cover your aquarium well. These fish are enormously good jumpers and it would be a shame if they were to jump out of your aquarium. It is best to have more females than males because the males are very keen to mate. Yet you can suddenly have more males in your tank than you put in yourself. This is because infertile female swordtails can very quickly "rebuild" themselves as males.

Cichlids

A cichlid is a bass-like fish that attaches a lot of importance to its own territory. Cichlids are phenomenal fish that have such an effect on some aquarium owners that they have specialised in the

with three well-known members. The Cardinal Tetra is a fish of four centimetres in length and it weighs about 1.5 grams. This red-blue fish looks particularly beautiful if you have an aquarium with a dark backing. The Cardinal Tetra originally comes from the Amazon area. All tetras swim in schools, but it is often sufficient to have six of them. The Neon Tetra can also grow to four centimetres and does not weigh more than a gram. Amateurs mix up the Cardinal Tetra and the Neon Tetra. Emperor Tetras are somewhat larger (6 centimetres) and often salmon coloured. Tetras thrive in all water layers and you can combine them well with other types of fish. They are relatively simple fish to keep and many beginners choose the above-mentioned sorts.

keeping of solely this type of fish. They are not the easiest fish to keep, which is why beginners are advised against them. The cichlid family is large and there are some real brutes amongst them. But if you still want to keep cichlids, you should consider the Angel Fish and the Purple Cichlid. The Angel Fish is a large fish of about 15 centimetres and it therefore also requires a suitably large tank. If your aquarium contains less than 80 litres of water then you are not doing this fish a favour. Angel Fish can sometimes reach a height of 25 centimetres. Therefore it goes without saying that the aquarium tank must also be suitably high to give this stately fish a home. The Purple Cichlid is a real "caveman", which means that you must give the animal a chance to make a cave. For this, put half a coconut or a flower pot in your aquarium. This fish, which comes from West Africa, is about 5 centimetres smaller than the Angel Fish. The Blue Ram is probably one of the easiest cichlids to keep. This 6 centimetre long fish comes from South America. If you are going to keep a Blue Ram you must make sure that you have some flat stones in your aquarium. Should you decide to keep these animals it is best to buy several females. We advise against several males. Blue Rams live on the ground, but they are less suitable for smaller aquariums. Although they themselves are not so large, they like

living in surroundings where there is enough room for several hiding places. Blue Rams have extended fin rays on the dorsal fin of the males. They get on very well with other types of fish and that is probably the reason that they are found in many community aquariums.

Mexican Swordtail

Swordtail

Harlequin Rasbora
(Rasbora heteromorpha)

Tiger Barb *(Barbus tetrazona)*

Red Zebra

The Red Zebra is a fish that can often be found in the special Malawi aquarium. They are fairly big fish, as they can grow to 10 centimetres. The females have given this type its name: They are often orange-red in colour with horizontal stripes on their bodies. Males can sometimes even be blue all over. Red Zebras live in the bottom and middle zones of your aquarium. Although this is not a fish that is particularly suitable for beginners, it goes well in a tropical community aquarium.

Barbs

The Harlequin Rasbora can often be found in tropical aquariums. This little fish of 3 centimetres in length lives in schools and it is a surface fish. You need a medium-sized aquarium for this fish. The Harlequin Fish is a busy little creature that needs a lot of room to swim in. The Lenbar is characterised by a dark stripe over its whole body. The fish originates in Asia and can easily reach 7 centimetres in length. The Rosy Barb is orange-yellow with a bit of black. It is not suitable for smaller aquariums because it can reach a length of 15 centimetres. The Purple-headed Barb owes its name to the fact that most of the colour of its body is on its head. This fish is about 6 centimetres long and lives in schools. If you put it in your aquarium, you will quickly notice that it prefers to swim in the middle zone. The Cherry Barb is a black-golden fish with orange-coloured fins which prefers to swim in the middle of your aquarium. It grows to 5 centimetres in length and lives in small schools. The Sri Lankan Two-spot Barb has a beautiful body that glows as if on fire. This fish also swims in schools and in the central zone. It grows to 3-4 centimetres in length. The Red-tailed (black) Barb is sometimes quite rightly known as the "fire-tail". This oblong fish with a brown-black colour has a bright orange tail. It is a relatively large fish of 12 centimetres in length and it needs a large aquarium with lots of hiding places. It is a solitary fish, so you should only buy one. The fish flourishes best at the bottom of your aquarium where it can search for food. Most barbs like a relatively closely planted aquarium.

Penguin Fish

The little fish with the tell-tale name of Penguin Fish can be found in many new aquariums. This fish can grow to about 6 centimetres and has a black line, which runs from its head to the point of its tail. You have to keep these fish in a school, and you must also ensure that you have lots of plants.

Black Molly

These jet-black fish are about 6 centimetres long. They originated in Mexico. This fish is one of the

Penguin Fish
(Thayeria boehlkei)

Black Molly
(Poecilia sphenops)

Glowlight Tetra
(Hemmigramus erythrozonus)

Leopard Cory
(Corydoras leopardus)

live-bearing fishes. Black Mollies are very easy to breed but they are not always simple to keep. This is because they are very susceptible to diseases. White spot occurs fairly often (see also the chapter Feeding, Health and Care).

Glowlight Tetra

The Glowlight Tetra is a small fish (3 centimetres) from South America. It is best kept in a school of about 8-10 in your aquarium. It is not a difficult fish to keep as long as you just have some plants in your aquarium where it can find shelter. These fish swim a lot and that is why it is best to put them in an aquarium with plenty of room. The Glowlight Tetra is well known for its tranquillity and good nature. Although they are middle-zone fish, they can often be seen swimming at the bottom. Glowlight Tetras are fairly shy and that means that they sometimes do not get enough food. In that case you must feed them separately.

Catfish (Corydoras family)

Many types of fish go under the name of catfish. We would easily be able to fill this little book with them, which is why we are restricting ourselves to the most well-known group among the catfish: the corydoras family. This family is very big. They originated in South America and they stand out because of their striking shape. These catfish have broad heads with barbels and the rear part of the body runs conical right up to the tail. They are true ground inhabitants and they love searching for food on the ground with their snouts. This is called "up-ending". If you keep these fish you must make sure that you have very fine substrate material. The corydoras are also real cleaners. All the food that lands on the ground is destined for them. By nature they search for worms on the bottom with their sensitive barbels. Their favourite place for doing this is in a sandy or clay substrate. You can, however, also put gravel on the bottom of your aquarium, as long as it is round gravel. Gravel can also be bought in shops, but you must be careful. Often the gravel is made of broken glass and that can be very sharp. If your fish goes up-ending, the barbels can be damaged and sometimes even amputated. The barbels are one of the most important sensory instruments of the sheat fish and the animal cannot exist without them. The corydoras have an extra respiratory organ and you will see the fish regularly go to the surface for a breath of air. They do this to replenish the supply of air in their intestines so they can also survive in an environment that is low in oxygen. Corydoras prefer to live in schools and most members of the corydoras family are about 2.5 centimetres long. You can keep whole groups of them but you

Panda Cory
(Corydoras panda)

Arched Cory
(Corydoras arcuatus)

Pearl Gourami
(Trichogaster leeri)

Honey Gourami
(Colisa chuna)

must take the size of your tank into account. If you buy these fish, make sure that only one type of corydoras are together in the plastic bag or container. In a stress situation these fish can emit a substance which is fatal for other types of fish. Therefore be very careful. Common corydoras which are great for keeping in small tropical aquariums are the Tail Spot Pygmy Cory (3 centimetres), the *corydoras habrosus* and the Dwarf Corydoras. The latter do not grow longer than 2 centimetres.

Paradise Fish
Some experienced aquarium owners think that Paradise Fish are not suitable for beginners. These relatively large fish (10 centimetres) need a lot of space and therefore they are definitely not suitable for a small tank. They are very active fish and they can even become very aggressive towards their own kind. Paradise Fish require their own territory. But they go very well in a tropical aquarium.

Gouramis
Different types of gouramis can be bought in the shops. The Honey Gourami is suitable for a beginner's aquarium. These fish originated in China and grow to about 5 centimetres in length. They live in schools. Both the female and the male Honey Gourami are beautiful to behold. During the period of courtship, which precedes the

mating, the male displays his beautiful dark blue-black breast and he becomes honey-orange in colour. The dorsal fin is yellow. It is a beautiful, colourful fish for your aquarium. The Honey Gourami is a surface fish.

The Diamond Gourami is different altogether. This Asiatic fish can grow to 12 centimetres and therefore it is less suitable for a small aquarium. It owes its name to the thousands of little diamonds, which seem to sparkle on its body. Males have an orange chest and an extended dorsal fin. The Diamond Gourami is great for keeping in pairs and with their stately bearing they will emanate a great deal of tranquillity in your aquarium.

Dwarf Gourami
(Colisa lalia)

The Chocolate Gourami (5 centimetres) can be kept in a smaller aquarium. This fish lives in small schools and owes its name to its brown coloured exterior. The Dwarf Gourami and the Pygmy Gourami have similar names but this is one of the few similarities. The 4- centimetre long Pygmy Gourami comes from China and has an elongated bluish body. It is a surface fish. The Dwarf Gourami is two centimetres longer and can be found in the whole of Asia. Its body is much plumper and more colourful. The Striped Gourami is also colourful and comes from Asia. It is longer than its dwarf cousin; it can grow to 10 centimetres.

Blue Gourami
(Trichocastor trichopterus)

Siamese Fighting Fish
(Betta splendens), male

Common Hatchetfish
(Gasteropelecus sternicla)

The Sunset Gourami is a fish that sometimes seems to be swimming on its head. This impression is increased by the position of its snout, which points upwards. That means that it is a surface fish. This type of gourami can grow to 5 centimetres and prefers to live in small schools.

The Giant Gourami is absolutely not suitable for a beginner's aquarium. This fish grows to 80 centimetres and that means that you have to have an enormous aquarium. In tanks with less than 450 litres this beautiful fish would surely pine away.

Siamese Fighting Fish (Betta)

Along with the guppy and the goldfish this is probably one of the most well known fish. It comes from South-East Asia and grows to about 7 centimetres. You can buy them in the most beautiful colours. Salmon-pink, bright red or beautifully purple. The males also have very beautiful fins. It is relatively easy to keep female fighting fish. They live in small schools in the central zone of your aquarium. Males are a little more aggressive and it is best to keep them separate. If two males meet each other, a fight for life or death ensues. It is unnecessary to add that in this case not much is left of their beautiful fins. This is where it gets its name from: Siamese Fighting Fish.

Black-winged Hatchetfish

The Black-winged Hatchetfish is a fish that is kept in relatively many small tropical aquariums (minimum 45 litres). This fish is about 3.5 centimetres long and it weighs about 1.5 grams. It is a surface fish with a very striking body shape. If you want this fish in your aquarium, you must buy at least 10, because they live in schools.

Dwarf Rasbora

This middle-zone fish of about 3 centimetres in length is a fine asset for your beginner's aquarium. This oblong fish is orange with black round spots and golden stripes. It has a disproportionately large eye. The females often grow bigger than the males and here too you must buy a school of them.

Fish that you do not want in your aquarium

There are types of fish that are best not to have in your aquarium, unless you only keep this one type. An example is the Tiger Fish. This fish comes from Africa and is renowned for its gluttony. In nature this sort of fish has an important role, in that it eats weak and sick fish. But in your aquarium all types of fish must be able to live alongside each other. Compare it with a swimming pool full of people. You do not put a great white shark in it ...

Scissor Tail Rasbora
(Rasbora trilineata)

Bleeding Heart Tetra
(Hyphessobrycon erythrostigma)

Kissing Gourami
(Helostomia temmincki)

The plants

Not only when buying fish but also when buying plants you must be well prepared for your task. Over-impulsive purchases are to be avoided in this case too. Make sure that you have decided on which plants go well in your aquarium.

There are a few tips and tricks to be borne in mind. Furthermore, in this chapter, you will find information about plants that you can put in your tropical community aquarium.

Plants that grow above water
Many plants for aquariums will grow above the water surface. Always ask about this when you buy some. The reason is that the leaves that are above water will disappear. The speed at which this process takes place is dependent on the type of plant. As soon as a new underwater leaf is formed, you must remove the lowest old leaf.

Plants in pots with stonewool
Some plants can be bought in little pots that have stonewool in

them. Never put these pots into your aquarium as they are. First remove the pot and the stonewool very carefully from the plants. After this rinse the roots out and pay attention to irregularities. In this way you can prevent uninvited guests, such as bloodsuckers, from ending up in your aquarium. Always plant the plants apart from each other, so that they cannot suffocate each other. Never forget to remove the lead tab that is supplied with the plant, as lead is poisonous.

Swamp plants and water plants
It is useful to be able to tell the difference between the two sorts. Swamp plants are plants that can survive both above and under water. Water plants on the other

hand can only live under water. Swamp plants are sold more often than water plants. This is because they are easier to grow. Many water plants are imported from countries such as Singapore.

A swamp plant can look quite different in the shop than you had imagined. Most swamp plants undergo a metamorphosis when they are put in an aquarium. Some change the shape of their leaves, others change colour and still others change both the shape of their leaves and colour.

Although a swamp plant can survive both under and above water, it will have to get used to a life under water. It must switch over. The leaves with which it breathed above water are not suited for underwater breathing. As soon as new leaves appear, you must remove the older ones. Often they have already rotted away by themselves. Give your plants time to change and do not discard of them prematurely.

Purifying plants

Plants produce oxygen, which is required by fish (and other animals). They do it by consuming nutrients (see also the chapter about the chemistry of water). The coontail is a well-known, very purifying plant. This means that it can produce enormous amounts of oxygen, which is why it is sometimes called an oxygen plant. This is, of course, not quite justified, because every plant produces oxygen, unless it is made of plastic or is dead.

Green Lotus

Large Cognac Plant
(*Ammania gracilis*)

House plants

There are some shops which sell house plants for the aquarium. But this can never work, even though the shopkeeper will say otherwise. These house plants may be suitable for terrariums, but that is of course something completely different. A house plant will drown in an aquarium. During the drowning process some plants can even emit poisonous substances with all the attendant negative consequences.

Cabomba furcata

Placing a plant in the aquarium

The place of the plant in the aquarium depends on two things. First, there is of course your personal taste. What do you think is beautiful? On the other hand you have to take the form and the size of the plant into account. There are low-growing plants that are suitable for the foreground or the middle zone.

High-growing plants should be placed at the back of the aquarium or in a corner. Try to plant the plants in groups. Pay attention to the differences in the shape and colour of the leaves and try to distribute this. Here too, too much can be a bad thing. The rule of thumb is that for every ten centimetres of front glass there should be one type of plant in the tank. So an aquarium that is 60 cm wide offers space for six types of plants. Choose plants that do not grow too large.

Plants and light

The flourishing of plants depends to a large extent on the lighting in your aquarium. This must be very good. Fluorescent lamps are often used for the lighting, but remember that not every fluorescent lamp is suitable for an aquarium. Ask in the specialist shop or an experienced aquarium owner for advice. When you have advanced a little more with your hobby, you will notice that some plants are very sensitive to the type of light. So not only the amount of light is important (expressed in watts), as some plants flourish in blue and red lighting.

Types of plants

Just as in the case of the fish we are also going to discuss some types of plants which can be kept very well in a tropical aquarium. Because aquarium owners often use the Latin names, we will also give these, in brackets.

Red Telanthera (*Telanthera 'lilacina'*) and Scarlet Hygro (*Althernathera reineckii 'roseafolia'*)

The Red Telanthera is a stem plant with dark-red leaves. This is a typical above-water plant during the growing phase, so it can look different when you buy it. This telanthera needs quite a bit of light, so do not place it in a dark corner. If you did this, the plant would not become nice and red and additionally it would then be

Red Parrot Leaf
(*Alternathera rosea-folia*)

easy prey for algae. It is best to place the Red Telanthera in the middle of the tank but make sure that you do not put too many of them together. The same is true for the Scarlet Hygro. This little brother has red-coloured shoots on its leaves, which makes the whole thing look somewhat more colourful. The Scarlet Hygro is a swamp plant that does not think much of cold feet. Floor-heating can prevent this.

Red Ammannia
(Ammannia senegalensis or Ammannia diffusa)
The Red Ammannia is also a typical example of a plant that can look different in the shop than in

*Ammannia
senegalensis*

Ruffled Sword Plant
*(Aponogeton
crispus)*

your aquarium. Under water it can have beautiful cognac-coloured leaves. In aquariums in shops it often looks green and fleshy. This swamp plant needs a good deal of lighting. It is best to put it in the middle of your aquarium, depending of course on the height of the plant you have bought. It can grow to a maximum height of 40-45 cm. The Ammannia is easy to propagate. You just cut the tips off and, after planting, new roots will quickly form. But it is not the easiest plant for your aquarium and it is sometimes very sensitive to algae. So you need green fingers for this one.

Ruffled Sword Plant
(Aponogeton crispus)
This water plant originated in Sri

Lanka. It is a very easy plant, which can strongly be advised for beginners. It is not particularly sensitive to light, although too much light can cause growth. The Ruffled Sword Plant also does not bother too much about the water it is put into, as it adjusts to it easily. Often a single plant is enough in your aquarium. The leaves can grow to 25-40 cm in length and they are sometimes up to 5 cm wide.

Giant Babies' Tears
(Bacopa amplexicaulis)
Giant Babies' Tears is a swamp plant which was originally found above or in shallow waters in the coastal regions of the Atlantic Ocean, but also in the middle of the United States. It is not really a difficult plant but it needs to be well lit. It does not make much of a fuss as far as the water is concerned, but, just as in the case of many tropical plants, the water should not be too acidic. It is a stem plant with leaves of about 2 cm long and 1.5 cm wide. They can grow to quite a height: 60 cm. Giant Babies' Tears thrive in the middle, or at the back of your aquarium. Its brother is the Large-leafed Bacopa. This plant grows less high (50 cm). They are green plants, but if you give them too much light they can go brown. It is best to put these plants in a little group so that the narrow stems do not get lost amongst the other plants.

Cabomba *(Cabomba aquatica and Cabomba piauhyensis)*

We will discuss two sorts of cabomba here: the red and the green. The Green Cabomba can grow very high, but it will usually keep to the height of your aquarium. The Red Cabomba closely resembles its brother and can reach 60 cm. It is a real water plant and therefore it prefers not to come above the surface. The cabomba is a stem plant with very finely branching leaves. It is a delicate plant that you should not put in your aquarium if you have busy fish. Cabombas do not like to be transplanted and you have to put them in soft water. All in all the cabomba is not the first choice for a beginner. If you do go for it, put the plant in the middle or at the back of your aquarium. Remember good lighting.

Coontail *(Ceratophyllum demersum)*

The Coontail is a plant that is often unjustifiably called the oxygen plant. It is very often seen in tropical aquariums and is also easy to keep. It makes few demands. It is a plant for the background because it can easily reach 1.5 m in length. The Coontail is an annual water plant that dies off in the autumn. It does not need much light, but it needs the right light. If that is okay, then you can enjoy a fresh green plant for a year.

Green Cabomba
(Cabomba aquatica)

Bacopa sp.

Red-brown Crypt
(Cryptocoryne petchii)

sometimes almost becomes black. It definitely brings a lot of atmosphere into your tank and, as long as you do not transplant it, it will do well. Its little brother *Nevillii* is the smallest member of the family. It closely resembles the large family member, but its leaves do not get longer than about 7 cm. If you choose a crypt, it is good to have floor heating. The position in the aquarium is also dependent on the type. The smallest ones are fine for the front of the aquarium, and the larger ones should be put more towards the back. You must pay special attention to the lighting. Luckily this type of plant has a built-in manual for this very purpose. If the leaves start pointing straight upwards, it is looking for light and is not getting enough. If the leaves are growing just above the ground, then they are hiding from the light because they are getting too much. You must get the balance right. Your fish are often happy about the presence of the crypt because they can find a hiding place in it.

Red-brown Crypt (Cryptocoryne petchii)

The plants of the cryptocoryne family originated in south-east Asia. The most common member in our aquariums is the Red-brown Crypt. The plant does not grow particularly high (22-35 cm), but it does get quite wide. Some leaves are 20 cm long. The plant has a bronze-brown colour, which

Amazon Sword (Echinodorus amazonicus)

This sturdy swamp plant is definitely not suitable for small aquariums. In spite of its size it is not a difficult plant. In order to keep its leaves nice and freshly green, you must make sure that the plants do not stand in direct (sun)light. A place at the back of the tank is just right for it.

Anacharis or elodea
(Elodea densa)

There are probably only a few beginners who have never tried the anacharis. It is a very popular beginner's plant because it demands relatively little from its surroundings. This water plant does, however, think it is nice if it gets a good deal of light. The lighting determines the colour of the leaves. These vary from very light green to very dark green. It is best to give the Anacharis a space at the back of your aquarium. Look after it well, as it has to be "pruned" regularly. If the conditions are good, it sometimes grows 15 cm a day. In its natural habitat it can reach a height of 4 m. A disadvantage of the Anacharis is the fact that the stem of the plant tends to go bald at the bottom if the plant grows very high.

Stargrass
(Heteranthera zosterifolia)

The light-green leaves of this easily grown swamp plant can sometimes grow to 5 cm. The length of the plant itself varies. It regularly grows right up to the surface of the water and floats on it. The plant is very suitable for the foreground of your aquarium if you take the tips off it every week. It branches quickly and profusely, so if you do not want to fill your whole aquarium with Stargrass, you must try to limit the growth. In doing so, try not to damage the leaves. Stargrass needs a lot of light. The more light, the brighter the green colour of the plant. The composition of the water is less important.

Water Pennywort
(Hydrocotyle leucocephala)

This plant is absolutely unsuitable as a foreground plant. It has a strong urge to the light and it will do its best to reach the surface of the water as quickly as possible. Once it has got there, the plant forms floating plants. In view of the fact that the lighting hood of many aquariums is also at the top,

Amazon Sword
(Echinidorus amazonicus)

Stargrass
(Heteranthera zosterifolia)

Hygro
(Hygrophila
polysperma)

If you choose this plant, put several in a group with each other. They do not need a great deal of light but if the light is not strong enough the green leaves can go brown. If the leaves go yellow and have spots, then the plant has an iron deficiency. Disadvantage of the plant: it can grow rampant. So from the beginning keep this plant in check by removing the tips on a weekly basis.

Water Wisteria
(Hygrophila difformis)
A Water Wisteria is also an example of a plant that looks completely different under water than above water. For you as a (future) aquarium owner the underwater version is of course the most important one. The underwater plant has a beautiful, finely branched leaf, whereas the above water version has leaves which strongly resemble those of a stinging nettle. This plant with light-green stems falls into the category of swamp plants. The Water Wisteria is particularly suitable for beginners, because it takes root fairly quickly, while other plants need more time for this. You must use a lot of light but be careful. The Water Wisteria has the tendency to grow towards the light. So put it in the middle of your aquarium so that it cannot grow crookedly. In addition you will have to attend to this plant regularly by taking out its tips. If you do not do this, the Water Wisteria will have no problem at

the plant will take away a lot of light in this manner. Fish that do not like light often seek the protection of the leaves of this plant. The Water Pennywort has light-green wavy leaves.

Hygro
(Hygrophila polysperma)
The Hygro is a strongly growing stem plant. This swamp plant can reach a height of about 60 cm. It is very suitable as background planting for a beginner's aquarium.

all in running riot over your whole tank and then "climbing" out of your aquarium.

Giant Ambulia and Dwarf Ambulia *(Limnophila sessilliflora)*

If you have room for a Giant Ambulia, you will have a real attention-grabber in your aquarium. If all conditions are as they should be, it can grow to 60 cm. The plant has 20 separate leaves which together form a crown that can look almost woolly. It is an ideal plant for the background. The lighting must be strong. The Giant Ambulia can grow enormously fast, sometimes 12 cm a day. If you plant this plant, it is advisable to do this in groups of about 10 plants each. Do not plant them too close to each other, otherwise they will not be able to develop their "crowns". The Dwarf Ambulia is also a suitable plant for beginners. Remember that you must be able to combine this plant with fish. If you have many fish that eat plants, you can quickly lose the Dwarf Ambulia, as it is a popular snack. Just like the Giant Ambulia the Dwarf Ambulia is light green in colour. It is fine to put this plant in the middle zone. Ambulias are real water plants.

Java fern *(Microsorium pteropus)*

Java fern is a plant that you must not put on the bottom. You must fix this swamp plant to stones, to back walls or to driftwood. If you do put it on the bottom, the plant will be dead in no time. The Java fern does not require much light. If it only has moderate light, it will not grow too fast but constantly. It is a super plant for the beginner and you can put it both in the middle and at the back of the aquarium.

Lotuses *(among others: Nymphaea lotus)*

There are 3 sorts of lotus which are suitable for a beginner's aquarium. They need quite a bit of light and that means that you must remove the longest leaves now and again, so that the whole plant can

Water wisteria *(Hygrophila difformis)*

King Tetra
(*Impaichtys kerry*)

get light. If you buy lotus plants in the shop, you will notice that they are little bulbs. Put them loosely on the bottom, then they will take root more quickly.

Lotuses are known as floating leaf plants. If you decide on a Green Tiger Lotus, it is best to only have a single plant. It owes its name to its grass green colour, on which

Red Lotus
(Nymphea lotus)

brownish spots can be seen. This lotus can grow to 30 cm in height, but it is above all the leaves that give this plant a majestic appearance. These leaves can grow to about 15 cm in length and width.

The Red Tiger Lotus has somewhat rounder leaves than its green namesake. It grows somewhat higher and wider than the green version. The Thai Lotus is also very easy to keep. It grows to about 15 cm high and its leaves sometimes have a diameter of 12 cm.

Common Bladderwort
(Utricularia vulgaris)

Just like the Java Fern, the Bladderwort is a plant that you should not plant at the bottom. Although this water plant is very popular, it is not easy to keep. That is why not many beginners choose Bladderwort. You can allow this plant to float or you can fix it to something, but you must have a glass-clear aquarium. The plant needs to be well lit, but over-lighting is often fatal. Bladderwort is fairly delicate and cannot survive in too high a temperature.

Green Lotus
(Nymphea lotus)

Algae

No book about aquariums would be complete without a chapter about algae. You will soon notice that algae fulfil a double role in your aquarium, and that is why it is useful to know the essentials about them.

Bronze Catfish
(Corydoras aneus)

In this chapter you will get information about the sorts of algae, their characteristics and how you can try to deal with them.

How do algae form?

Algae form at the moment that conditions are ideal for them. New lighting can cause algae, also a surplus of food in the aquarium. They can also occur when the water has not been changed for a long time or when you have bought new plants, which have traces of algae on them. It is important to find out what the cause is, so that you can do something about it. The easiest

way is to keep a logbook. In this logbook you should record all important things, for example:
- new lighting (note the date of purchase, colour and other information)
- purchase of apparatus
- purchase of fish (when, which ones, characteristics, other information)
- purchase of plants (ditto)
In this way you can not only see where something has perhaps gone wrong, but you can also use it to increase your knowledge about your hobby.

Thread algae

Thread algae are often found in recently started aquariums. If you have a lot of calcium in your tap water, the calcium will end up in your aquarium. This is a nutrient for the thread algae. Sometimes the presence of thread algae can be useful because they remove many (superfluous) nutrients from your aquarium. If you do not want

the thread algae, you must ensure that your water has the correct composition. In addition you must keep the water low in nutrients. The thread algae look a bit like seaweed and they are relatively harmless in your aquarium.

Beard algae

The beard algae is not a nice thing to have in your aquarium because it is so difficult to remove. It belongs to the group of red algae. If you have this form of algae in your aquarium, it is usually found on a plant. It is best to completely remove this plant from your tank. You can recognise the beard algae by its green-black threads, which can be long. They often hang from the edges of leaves.

Fuzz algae

Fuzz algae is a form of algae which looks very much like the beard algae. If you have fuzz algae in your aquarium you can be sure that your aquarium will be completely overgrown by it in next to no time. The algae often come with new plants. The best way to combat these algae, is with fish that eat them. The Mexican Highland Carp is a fish that loves to eat these algae. Feed these fish well otherwise they will also eat up your plants. You can buy the fish yourself or you can go and look at your local aquarium club. Many clubs loan out this sort of fish.

Banded Epiplatys
(Epiplatys dageti)

Regular water
change

Black brush algae

Black brush algae is a red algae and is, like the beard algae, difficult to remove from your aquarium. Here too you must take the plant with the algae on it out of your tank. Even though this type of algae is a red type of algae, the colour of the black brush algae does not look red. Black brush algae vary in colour from black to spinach-green. The red colour is hidden under this layer of "paint".

Brown algae

Brown algae are usually harmless. These algae can get everywhere - on the panes, on the stones, on apparatus that hangs in the aquarium, everywhere.

You can get rid of these algae with a tool that can be bought in specialist shops. Remember that by removing algae, you have not found out the cause for the appearance of the algae in your tank. In the case of brown algae, you must be economical with food and the water must have the right composition. You can also decide on leaving the algae where it is. It often happens that brown algae disappear by themselves when the aquarium has been properly "run in".

Blue algae

If there is blue algae in your aquarium, you will not be happy. It is a slimy form of algae. Fortunately you can remove blue

Platy

algae relatively easily. You can suck it out with a pipe (get advice at the specialist shop). Blue algae do not always look blue. Their colour can vary from blue to greenish, sometimes even black-brown. The algae can get almost everywhere. Usually they start at the bottom of your aquarium and cover the whole of it under a slimy layer. Blue algae can stink to high heaven. If you cannot suck the algae away with a pipe, you can try the following: first find the cause of the algae coming to your aquarium. In doing so you can put your logbook to good use. When you have found the cause, switch off the light in your aquarium for three days. Also hang a blanket over it, so that no light from outside can shine into the tank. Blue algae need light to exist. After three days you can get all the dead algae and rubbish out with a bucket. Slowly increase the light level again, every day a little longer. In this way your aquarium will get going again, slowly and peacefully. The plants will have a somewhat sickly appearance after three days of darkness but they will usually survive this okay.

Green algae

Green algae in your aquarium cannot do much damage. If you have green algae in your tank, it is even a sign that your water composition is probably good. The algae have greenish threads that are sometimes woven together. You can remove them very easily with your hand, or if you find this unappealing, you can roll them up on a Q-Tip. Get the green algae out of your aquarium because they use the same nutrients as your plants.

Other ways of dealing with algae

In addition to the special ways of dealing with each type of algae, there are also some general tips that we can give you. Never put your aquarium in bright sunlight. This will cause plants to use too many nutrients and a deficiency will ensue. This is an invitation to the algae. When you buy plants you must first examine them to see if they have algae. If as a beginner you are in doubt as to whether you will be able to recognise the algae, take an experienced aquarium owner with you for the purchase.

Algae also flourish if you do not change the water in time. Depending on the size of your tank it is best to change a fifth part of the water every week. Never change all the water at one go, unless you want to start your aquarium completely afresh. If the plants in your aquarium are growing well, they will allow little room for algae. So make sure that the plants are given excellent growing conditions. That means that you must ensure sufficient nutrients and sufficient light.

Proper light is very important

Food, health and care

Keeping an aquarium is a living hobby. That means that every day you are dealing with living creatures. Fish and plants, you must care for them both and keep them in good health.

Red Tailed Black
Shark
(Labeo bicolor)

Without your help the animals will die and the plants will wither. So it is wise to know how best to feed the fish, how to care for your aquarium and what you must do if there is disease in your aquarium. You will find all these points in this chapter.

The natural habitat
Your fish and plants will best flourish if you try to imitate their natural habitat as well as possible. That means that you must ensure that the water composition is correct and the temperature is not too high. You can get information about most fish and plants that are suited to a beginner's aquarium. Find out what the eating habits of the fish are, and try to provide for these. For plants it is important that you know which fish eat plants.

Daily check
Check daily if your fish are still in a good condition. If they are playful and/or they display mating behaviour, you can be sure that they are in good health. But if a fish withdraws, you must find out what is going on. It could be that you have recently introduced a new fish into your aquarium and that this fish appears to be fairly dominant. If another fish withdraws as a result of this, this does not mean that it is sick, but rather subordinate. In another case it can well be a disease or perhaps your fish is already old.

Dominant and subordinate
Some fish are so dominant that they do not even give other fish the chance to eat something. You must pay special attention to this,

otherwise the subordinate fish may starve. If you have to deal with this situation, you must carefully target when feeding. Surface inhabitants will then often get dried food and bottom inhabitants will get food tablets. There are other ways of doing this, but that is in part dependent on the sort of fish you are dealing with.

Water layers and food

Earlier on in this book we explained that fish live in certain layers of water. This has a great influence on their eating habits. Animals at the bottom root for their food, which often consists of worms and larvae. Fish from the middle layers of water live on insects, such as mosquitoes, larvae or crustaceans such as water fleas. Surface inhabitants live on insects that live on the water or land on it. So you will understand that you cannot just buy a simple pot of dried food.

The amount of food

Some fish can literally kill themselves eating. So never give them too much food. There is often already enough food in the aquarium, for example: the eggs one type of fish lays are a real treat for other fish.
Cardinal Tetras are well known as egg-thieves. Guppies, Black Mollies, and other fish like eating algae. Although it is dependent on the fish in your aquarium, you can keep to the following rule of thumb. Feed the fish at intervals of at least two days. Make sure that these are small portions, so that no food remains on the bottom, which can cause pollution.

Types of food

There are three types of food that you will have to deal with if you want to maintain a flourishing community tank. There is live food, which consists of living things, such as mosquito larvae and water fleas. Frozen food can be bought in the pet shop and there is the well-known dried food.

Live food

Live food can often be purchased in good specialist aquarium shops. There are aquarium owners who catch their live food themselves from ditches. If you also decide to do this, always use a white bucket. With a white bucket you can see precisely what you have caught, and in this way you prevent possible uninvited guests from entering your aquarium. Some examples of live food, which are often used, are water fleas and copepods. These are very popular. In addition there are various sorts of mosquito larvae. Red Mosquito larvae are the larvae of the blood-worm. If you set out to catch water fleas, you will come across white mosquito larvae. These are the larvae of a mosquito which does not bite and which can be recognised by its transparent body.

The White Mosquito larvae can be bought in specialist aquarium shops in tubes that are filled with water and larvae. The larvae can live for quite a while without oxygen or food and so can be easily kept in a tube. You have to be careful with Black Mosquito larvae. These larvae come from the Northern House Mosquito, which bites. Do not take too many of these home; before you know it you will have a plague of mosquitoes.

Frozen food

Almost all live food can also be bought in frozen form. As a beginner it is best to use this because in this way you do not run the risk of introducing irregularities into your aquarium. Yet there is also a definite disadvantage to frozen food. Your fish will not be encouraged at all to go hunting, although that is in their nature.

Dried food

Dried food can be purchased in many types and sizes. The disadvantage of dried food is that it usually floats. Some fish gobble the food up at the surface and in so doing take in so much air that it lands in their intestines. Your fish will then start "belching".

*Aphyosemion
coeleste*

You can avoid this by wetting the food before you sprinkle it into your aquarium.

Fish diseases

One of the negative things about keeping an aquarium is the possibility of disease breaking out in your tank.

The most well known fish disease is called **White Spot**. White Spot is a parasite that is present in many aquariums. A healthy fish can put up resistance to it. If there is a fish in your aquarium with reduced resistance, however, the parasite can lodge on it. If that

happens the parasite immediately starts reproducing itself. These offspring can then "attack" healthy fish too and so cause an explosion of disease. A "medicine" which kills the parasites can be bought in shops. It is usually given as a course over several days.

Another disease is **Rust** or **Gold Dust Disease** (Oödinium). If your fish has this disease, it looks as if it is sprinkled with rust or gold dust. You can buy preparations in the shops to combat this disease. These too are given as a course over several days.

Tuberculosis can also occur in your aquarium tank. You can recognise it by bulging eyes, swellings on the body or growths. As soon as you see this on a fish, you must remove the fish from your aquarium. If you do not do this and the fish dies, the other fish will start nibbling at it and then they will also be infected.
If the tuberculosis is already at an advanced stage, it is best to decontaminate the whole aquarium. Unfortunately there is still no medicine against tuberculosis in the shops. Always try to prevent contamination. Even if you only have a little wound, the bacteria can still infect you. If you have health problems (inflammation or suchlike), tell your doctor immediately that you have an aquarium. This can save the doctor a great deal of searching.

Aphyosemion australe

Addresses

Black Neon
*(Hybhessobrycon
herbertaxelrodi)*

Association of Aquarists
Sec (AP),
2 Telephone Road, Portsmouth,
Hants, England.

British Cichlid Association
Ken Hilton, 248 Longridge
Knutsford, Cheshire, WA16 8PH,
England.
Telephone +44 (0)1565 633318.
Email memsec@bca.zetnet.co.uk.

British Discus Association
F.W. Ashworth, 41, Pengwern,
Llangollen, Clwyd. LL20 8AT
UK.

British Killifish Association
A. Burge
14, Hubbard Close, Wymondham,
Norfolk NR18 ODU, England.
Tel 0953-607004.

**Catfish Association of Great
Britain**
Andy Stratton, 25 College Road,
Haywards Heath, W Sussex RH16
1QN, England.

**Goldfish Society of Great
Britain**
Ms. Christine Griffin, 23 Green
Lane, Northgate, Crawley, West
Sussex RH10 2JX, England.

**International Marine Aquarist
Association**
Secretary, IMAA
P.O.Box 7, Ilminster, Somerset
TA19 9BY, England.

Marine Conservation Society
9 Gloucester Road, Ross-on-Wye,
Herefordshire HR9 5BU, fax
011-441-989-567815.

Internet

A great deal of information can be found on the internet. A selection of websites with interesting details and links to other sites and pages is listed here. Sometimes pages move to another site or address. You can find more sites by using the available search engines.

Butterfly (Ram)
Cichlid
(Microgeophagus ramirezi)

www.aquahobby.com
Huge aquarium website full of fish keeping information.

www.aqualink.com
US site, general fish keeping information and links.

www.aquariumhobbyist.com
US hobbyist site, general fish keeping information and links.

fins.actwin.com/index.php
Huge list of fishy links and helpful advice.

**www.fishkeeping.co.uk/
index.php**
This website has been designed as a comprehensive guide to the fish keeping hobby, providing information to novice fish keepers and professional ichthyologists alike.

www.fishlinkcentral.com
A guide to aquarium resources on the internet.

www.fishgeeks.com
Here you can find information like fish profiles, articles, chat, encyclopedia, links and more.

www.bristolzoo.org.uk/what-tosee/aquarium/index.html
An online aquarium from Bristol Zoo.

www.londonaquarium.co.uk
One of Europe's largest exhibits of aquatic life.